All Darkness and Dahlias

ashley jane

illustrations by *Angie Shea*

all darkness and dahlias

Copyright © 2019 Ashley Jane
Cover Art © 2019 Nadiya Saara El-Sharkawy
Illustrations © 2019 Angie Shea

Ashley Jane - BreathWords
Alabama, USA
www.breathwords.com

All rights reserved. No part of this publication may be reproduced, distributed, or transmitted in any form or by any means, without prior written permission, unless for the purposes of reviewing.

Author's Note: This is a work of fiction. Locales and public names are sometimes used for atmospheric purposes. Any resemblance to actual people, living or dead, or to businesses, companies, events, institutions, or locales are completely coincidental.

All Darkness and Dahlias/
ashley jane 1st Edition
ISBN 978-1-7325327-2-4

ashley jane

this book is for the ones with dark hearts,
the seekers of chaos,
the ones who chase after shadows
and dance with ghosts

it's for the parts of you
that dwell behind the curtain

Contents

Dahlias   9

Demons   49

Danger   95

Darkness   135

Disillusion   167

Foreword

In a world of pretty verses that capture our imagination, Ashley Jane is a master. Armed with her extensive vocabulary and insight into the human mind, Ashley Jane sings us lullabies, allowing the reader to understand and feel complicated emotions.

Reading "All Darkness and Dahlias", I found a cadence that made each word flow and demand more. I am in awe of this lady's talent. Each poetry book she publishes goes deeper and finds a home in my thoughts.

- Gypsy Mercer, author of Into the Fire

I will forever be a fan of this writer. Each book keeps getting deeper, layer by layer. I love her talent and the way she speaks the words upon my heart. I cannot recommend this writer enough. She writes poetry the way it's meant to be felt.

- Alfa, author of I Find You in the Darkness

all darkness and dahlias

we become swallowed up in the night
as shadows bend and contort,
the luscious darkness calling our name

all darkness and dahlias

Dahlias

I am a forest, and a night of dark trees: but he who is not afraid of my darkness, will find banks full of roses under my cypresses.

Frederick Nietzsche

write me

poetry

wrapped

up in

decadent

black

velvet

poetry

ashley jane

communication lines

made from a string of stars,
whispers tied together with red, silk thread,
celestial lightning sparks
transmitting white noise
answered only by the breathless hush
of unfinished conversations
on lonely nights
we are the wild ones whispering
to the other side of night,
speaking in secret code to the ghosts
in the language of darkness

(10-22 -- for now, over and out)

words,

too long settled
in hollow bones,
pour like
poisoned honey
from our lips
we spill
madness and memories
that taste like something from long ago
we speak of smooth charmers
with gun slinger smiles
and discuss all the ways
our hearts led us astray
we sip on nostalgia and cheap wine,
recklessly flirting with the past
and all those things that didn't last

(we've always liked reminiscing)

ashley jane

we chanted spells,
practiced divination
at the edge of night,
stitched our secrets into a shadowed sky
we bowed at the altar of an indigo dark,
left violets and voodoo dolls
as offerings to the stars
while chasing mystic spirits betwixt and between,
our gypsy souls summoning
the wild and unseen

(*we need new company*)

we rise with the moon,
madness and chaos beneath our skin,
hellbent hearts caught up in the tide again
our light is reflected in the crashing waves
while distilled darkness runs in our veins
we are the shadows that shimmer

(*we are all that glitters*)

the fog is rising against bruised skies,
ghostly trails of smoke
staining the blackest nights
and we are wrapped up in the dark decadence,
our moon souls evoking celestial transcendence,
midnight opals morphing
into fantastical creations,
galaxies of glimmering lights
forming constellations,
the wind expertly mimicking
the darling wolf's call,
magic in the air as we watch the stardust fall

(*we are bathed in the shimmer*)

we were honest
about our darkness,
the way it protects us
with the most sublime shadows

we are soft silhouettes
in brutal light,
ruby whispers against
onyx skies

(*a kiss of day wrapped up in night*)

we sang of hope
in haunted places
and let beauty bloom
in the shadows
of ghosts

these nights are disturbingly pretty,
the smooth-soothing-glimmer
of gossamer raven wings,
a city of twilight
dressed in a veil of dreams

we sip elysian elixir
until heaven pours through our veins
and follow starlit paper trails
to travel through time,
waltzing through galaxies of shine
and shadows that move
like a slow-floating-diaphanous dark

we cross the bridge where the crows sing,
talking with the moon until morning comes,
and it all falls apart

(*we were not made for early days*)

we fancied it up,
dressed it in
midnight and marigold,
let it sink skin-deep,
all wicked need bathed in
pretty poisoned dreams
we declared its brilliance,
called it visual poetry,
icy hearts drenched in euphoria flames,
a warm blue inferno softly chanting our name

*(we fell for the burnt fire sunlight
with a full moon taste)*

cloud swirls paint abstract beauty
across darkened skies
midnight truths fly free as a bird,
shattering looking glass memories
until all that's left are figments
floating in the mind of dreamers

(*let us dream*)

i am

drawn to

souls

that hold

exquisite

darkness

she is blanketed by the night,
wrapped up in jasmine
and demure seduction,
hypnotized by the way it calls out to her

she may have a butterfly heart,
but her soul is a black sparrow

(*sometimes, her dark demands to fly*)

ashley jane

she consults late at night
with the wide-eyed stars,
whispering knife
and dagger secrets
under the cover of the dark
while the moon softly smolders,
searing itself into the sky
and she spills magic spells,
creating chaos from the quiet

(*she is all diamonds and danger*)

she painted roses over gray skies,
had a love affair with the blackest night,
created shadows that filled the air
she spilled stories in onyx and bone white
and danced with ghosts under moonlight,
but when the sun rose,
it was like she was never there

(*she made darkness seem like a graceful endeavor*)

her poetry is littered
with ghosts and bones,
with madness
buried in shallow graves,
with stars that shine
through the shadows

(will you read her?)

raven-eyed magic

in a shadow crow soul,
a thousand eyes
stand mesmerized
she is twisted candle lines that drip,
alchemy brewed up in fallen wax slips,
a thousand pulses pounding from within
an oak and cauldron heart,
bones that rattle in the pitch-black dark
like a sliver of echoes
shivering through the night,
or a rain of chimes falling
from navy skies

(*she is all dark magic beauty*)

somber, flint stone spark,
moments burning in the dark
she becomes the night

she is dagger and spell
weaving tales of war and peace,
letting pretense fall to the floor
she has the gift of magic
shackled to the night's roar,
and for you,
with your anxious breaths,
she weaves stories of dawn and death
as she channels her power
from fallen angels and rising witches
that live within the dark's richness
in blinding shadows, she communes
with ghosts and sorcery
and mystic moon runes,
her wicked words wrapped up in a rhyme
that holds you tight and haunts your mind

(*but, when morning comes, you'll be fine*)

she is drawn to the darkness,
but caught in the flickering flames
of the stars
the skies are on fire,
and she is entranced by the flames
a waiting beauty within a world of wings,
wanderlust and witchcraft in her veins
she is swallowed up by the night,
wrapped in a cocoon
of shadows and light,
of moths and the moon

(she moves between the two)

moonlit madness,

a dangerous aphrodisiac
that shocks the senses
and turns bliss into a kiss
that tastes like copper and fear
she rules the dark here,
mixing virtue with vice,
stirring them together
with the edge of her knife
she cultivates chaos
in forgotten corners,
wicked magic
and sinister spells
wrapped up in shadows,
luring you in on wild nights
like whispers in the mist,
a hint of peril hidden in
a touch of forbidden promises

(the dark has never tasted so sweet)

she blends herbs into magic,
    soothes and severs
    with tinctures and traps

    she breathes promise into packets
    of lemongrass and larkspur

    she weaves farewells into sachets
    of honeysuckle and jimsonweed

but, which will she put under your pillow?

        (*sweet dreams*)

she is smoke and spark,
inkwell spells brewed in the dark,
parchment scored with markings
of steel-edged dreams,
the phoenix in her chest
threatening to break free
she whispers incantations
under bold moonlight,
weaving spells in the shadows cast
by a heart on fire
that burns far too bright

(*she is the blaze seen on dark nights*)

she isn't like those other girls,
the bubble-gum pink,
dripping diamonds and dreams girls
NO, NOT AT ALL
she is more winter night divine
than summer day shine
she mingles with monsters
and dances with darkness
she is fascinated with serial killers
and talks to the ghosts in the walls

(*i am just like her*)

a constant thrum
of dip-dyed darkness
and magic moments
wound and bound in clenched fists,
this chaos folded up
into a million shades of madness,
living in the silent hush between heartbeats

(do you hear it, too?)

beneath the rolling fog,
buried somewhere in the deep,
the truth we seek lies undefined
in swirls of hidden secrets
that our bones will NEVER find

(acatalepsy)

a night wrapped
in banshee arms
and sweet foreboding,
haunted houses on hills
now overrun with spirits
who speak in legends
and weave magic from myth
you'll find her here
amidst the tombstones,
in a cemetery filled
with dandelions
and dark wishes,
reading funeral rites
for an imperfect love,
heart crossed,
eyes closed,
the florets falling softly,
little mercies
from the passing ghosts

(*she will grow a garden from their gifts*)

we planted words
and watered them with honey,
our own little garden
of love, lies and lullabies

we watched them grow
side – by – side

we told ourselves
that love would survive

(*it was either bloom or die*)

darkness
  rose
up
  with
    the
wildflowers

taste my words,
dark shadows dripping from my lips
there is sunshine in my soul
but blood on my fingertips
and while the poetry that spills
may be bittersweet,
there are fairytale stories
wrapped in these serpent dreams

(there are worlds of both within me)

there are ravens in my heart,
sparrows in my mind and crows in my closet
and i've realized that i've a thing for darkness,
the escalating madness and insanity,
the way it flies between my thoughts
(my words bloom and ripen best in the shadows)
but the night never lingers long enough,
whispering its too soon goodbyes

(*one last kiss before it crumbles in the light*)

silence

and the slow sweep of light
you r i s e,
a shadow of jaguars dwelling
behind your midnight eyes
along with
the air of something wicked,
a familiar stranger from
beyond the veil
(kiss me, kill me)
you part the gloaming
with a twist of knowing
(k i s s m e)
and a deadly quiet
that steals my breath
(k i l l m e)
until nothing but darkness is left

(*it is my turn to rise*)

midnight prayers
rising up
from damp leaves

tongues dancing
skyward
in violet flight
destined for the descent

counting down to
V E R T I G O

blue jay souls
sweep and swoon
while wrecking wrens
reunite
with the earth

(do you feel the magic brewing?)

here,

in this bitter cold,
warmth and light hide
behind the sunwade
while ice holds dominion,
painting flowers in frozen fractals,
white rose promises
and ivory moonflower lies,
little snowflakes
in geometric shapes
spilling from dark skies

(*we paint the night in ice and beauty*)

half-moon halos flickering
on haunted nights
while clouds camouflage
imperfect skies,
hiding the storms that brew
behind the veil

(*the dark has such glorious S E C R E T S to tell*)

we bind ourselves with knots,
cast spells with mere whispers
while feeling their biting sting
we channel the magic,
letting the power sing
as we stand soul to soul
with all the midnight ghosts
in the midst of an unraveling
we chant beneath these ardent stars
on haunted nights
draped in the dark's velvet illusion

(*its ethereal energy is holding us tight*)

eyes wide,
we search the dark for signs of life,
feathered fancies flying on wings of illusion

we use the shadows to hide,
leaving us to play behind the mask of night

we moondance with hidden skeletons,
reveling in the music of the stars

(*we are children of the dark*)

we've twisted superstitions
into pretty little omens,
tossed them in these
tempestuous seas,
watched them rage,
the air stained
with a purple haze
while winds whisper
midnight incantations,
sordid spells spilling
within the crashing waves,
the clash of fate and faith
mixed with pouring rain,
our reflections found
in each falling drop,
whispered words uttered
as the ocean thrums

(*...something wicked this way comes*)

all darkness and dahlias

Demons

(Come in under the shadow of this red rock),
And I will show you
something different from either
Your shadow at morning striding behind you
Or your shadow at evening rising to meet you;
I will show you fear in a handful of dust.

T.S. Eliot, The Waste Land

we are

hearts served up
like a delicate dish,
our souls
simmering slowly
below the surface
we drain the words
from our veins,
and squeeze
the ink-filled letters
from our beating hearts

(*this is how we make poetry*)

we took a moonlit stroll with ghosts,
trespassed through a graveyard of memories
the past is coming up roses,
but we only feel the sting of the thorns
we are playing a dangerous game,
the shadows we follow leading us astray
our once ocean galaxy hearts
are now riding the waves of something dark,
and the current cuts like a blade

(we are one slice from sinking)

we swam across the blue,
somewhere off the coast of the storm,
souls swept away by the summer rains

we became casualties of the crashing waves,
pawns of the ocean's rage,
those pretty pools and violet seas
filled with doom and madness writhing beneath

-- AND WE SINK,
feeding the monsters in the dark, dark, dark
pieces and parts of our hungry, haunted hearts

(a feast fit for kings)

we decorated our wrists
in darling dandelion chains,
wound autumn asters into rings,
wore chrysanthemums in our hair
given to us by the ghosts that rose
from the flowerbeds each night

we saw ourselves as ruined,
as a bitter, broken before and after
and the flowers made it better
(they made it better, right?)
their pretty petaled perfection
is so much more pleasing
than broken hearts that forgot how to shine

we adorned ourselves
in golden secrets and silver thorns,
dressed our disasters in morning glories
we became experts at vanishing
into this carefully crafted beauty,
our waiting wishes left withering on the vine

we became the timeless repetition of
it's fine...
we're fine...
i'm fine...

(*we hide within a layer of lies*)

we climb into bed with our ghosts,
cozy up to the demons that whisper our name
we commune with darker things,
hiding away under sheets of shadows
in the afterlife
because we're too afraid to live in the present

(*we aren't cut out for this*)

ashley jane

we are chasing time
as it echoes through us,
a lingering resonance of reminders
blooming like desperate voices
all racing and resolute
and aching to stain the world with poetry
we tumble like falling petals
beneath a frosted sun,
no singing shimmer,
just the dying wisps of melancholy filled mums
twisted up and hidden within the ashes,
left on the grave of all the words
we never got to say

(*we bloom in muted shades*)

roses and lilies

caress words spilled from soft hearts
but i am dark corners and hard edges
purple dahlias live within my ribs,
and my soul key is shaped
like a mum

(plant me beside the snowdrops)

these feet of mine keep
s l i p p i n g
on galaxies
and i'm losing ground,
invisible scars weighing me down,
a coffin filled with catastrophe
but the only poison here is me
i suppose i should've known

(*i am my own worst enemy*)

too many late hours
with blood shot eyes
and insomnia knocking on the door,
crumpled and torn pages
littering the floor
like corpses
on my left and right,
personal demons
ripped out during long, hard nights
when i was left with words
and embers in my chest
so i wrote out an epitaph
in fire and gasping breaths,
my damaging dalliance with darkness
leaving no time for rest

(*no rest for the weary*)

ashley jane

i slip-slide down narrow pathways
searching for a daylight dazzling
inside this skin of mine,
a dangerous thing
in a world where shadows lure,
their darkness beckoning me to stray
i am too often
twilight dreaming red,
a blood moon calling from midnight skies,
a mirage of matter and memory
drifting on a guttural scream
this world inside my veins
leaves me hovering between
undone and comfortably numb

(*i am a lost soul aching for peace*)

it's closing time,
last call for lost souls and haunted minds
drinking death as a cure
while trying to outrun the night
they are sipping on spirits
to erase the scars on their hearts,
counting down the minutes
until morning overtakes the dark,
each tendril of smoke
wrapping them up in a starry haze
while they hide in these moments
as a means of escape

(but the feeling won't last)

these haunted rooms
feel more like vacant tombs,
and we move
like ghosts
trapped in hallowed spaces,
flickers of light
in the shadows of gods and monsters,
filaments floating somewhere between,
caught in the vicious cycle
of war and peace

we hover
in a shiver of silence,
souls free falling
in the perpetual quiet

(*we have madness in our veins*)

you chain yourself to the pain
and throw away the key
because the mere threat of joy
leaves you shaking
with a spine-chilling fear
you've made yourself a cage
from doubt and shadow,
too in love with the way the darkness drips
to ever venture back into the light

(you have always been a glutton for punishment)

she is mad nights filled with fantasy
while words are fired so callously,
creating amaranthine stains
on her pale skin,
innocence caught in the crossfire
of war and sin,
shot down by a bullet
with butterfly wings

(*a drive-by dance with tragedy*)

raven-eyed and dragon born,
lips that taste of roses, wrath and scorn,
a sea inside her guarded heart
filled with lucid dreams and waves of dark
while glitter runs through her veins in shards
like glass that cuts and tears apart,
leaving behind only pieces from dawn to dusk
for sunshine souls she doesn't trust

(*too many liars wear masks of light*)

spells spill from her lips
wax drips from her fingertips,
and we stand
imprisoned-unsteady-aghast
the sunlight is sinking,
and it might be our last
so we overdose on pretty words
that go unheard
and rise the day after death,
wrapped up in our own silence,
victims of her mellifluous violence
WE ARE DISCORD AND DISTRESS

(*we are madness and unrest*)

beasts tell lies,
charm hiding fierce wolf eyes
and lips that skillfully weave,
those sweet silken spindles creating a web of grief
she clings to moments bittersweet,
tangled up in the hunt,
the dark whispering omens in ancient tongues
while the raven watches her untethered soul
become caught in a net with nowhere to go,
deftly wrapped up in dread
but still searching for hope

(*she stills sees stars in empty skies*)

you made friends
with all the skeletons in the closet,
but now it's time
to set those ghosts free

the past rises up,
graveyard shadows
entrapped within yesterday's ache,
hope strangled by memory's chain
and i stand,
hands fisted and teeth clenched,
grounded by pain
and the sweet taste of crimson,
struggling to keep the gates closed
fear awakens the darkest parts of us,
AND THOSE MONSTERS HATE TO BE CAGED

(*they're banging against the door*)

i sip slow,
barely lucid
after nights weighed down
by ghostly shadow souls,
this morning concoction
made of their darkness
collected like stale coffee in a jar

i sip slow,
lost in flashbacks
of last night's dream
where i chased an elusive memory
of ME - YOU - US,
of the moment when we let it all
slip away

i
sip
slow
and let it fade

(*sip. sip. fade.*)

devilish,
the way death calls
without a word
right as i remember how to breathe
its slow-shrill-scraping
driving me to my knees
I SINK,
its hands pulling me under
while i demand release,
the thawing grip only letting go
when it's too late

(*that's the nature of the beast*)

there is a chill in the air here,
a cold that seeps into the bones
of ice-covered hearts too frozen to thaw

it is open season on the lonely

autumn always seeks the lost ones,
the souls one break from falling apart

we are stored on the shelf beside a jar of hearts,
tucked within a chest full of fragments that bleed
i am found there, within all the pieces,
petals of glass plucked from a field of memories,
a lovely mess of shattered edges,
hiding in a box of broken wings

i was once found in summer's shimmer,
wrapped up in the brilliance of the milky way
i bathed in the light of a magical moon
but now i am buried in this resounding solitude
with a heart that stutter-stop-stutters,
tangled up in the leaves
and their whirlwind flutter

i write messages on them,
turn my words into poetry
for the upcoming winter,
reminders for myself to find when it's time

(*i am coming to terms with the fact
that this season is my time for hibernation*)

silence lies

where shadows loom
and fear sleeps
between heart beats
as we stand
quietly suspended,
struggling to
catch our breath

(we are all gasp but no inhale)

we spent the night
dancing on graves,
listening to
the lost souls scream

we were
our own version of broken,
filled with
moments of madness,
becoming one
with the ghosts

(*we finally found our people*)

we bloom in dripping red,
our petals stained in blood and dreams
we are cluttered minds seeking clarity,
tossing out burning shards of memories
we are moonstruck dahlias chasing after disaster,
flowers that only form on the darkest of nights

(pretty plum petals in the dark)

dark beauty whispers
floating on a breath of ashes,
darling death
disguised as love
and lightning flashes,
silver echoes in the gloaming
softly kissed by the rain,
sundown shadows
taking a fall from grace
as uncertainty settles
beneath the skin,
mystery sweeping through,
wilder than the wind,
midnight's secrets caged
within the beautiful decay
before thoughts are torn
from the storm,
their broken wings making an escape

(fly away, birdie)

we scavenge,
recovering thoughts from the bottom
of back alley hearts

we dig in the dark,
robbing from glass coffins
that shatter in our hands,
smearing words on our cheeks
like war paint from the deep

we search for life and death,
pulling out the emotions
long buried in our chest,
letting them bleed like ink,
spreading on the page

(*we are a trapped bird no longer caged*)

i saw you smolder,
a body in flames
within a world on fire,
my own blaze negating
all those whispered lies
of precious moments
under pink diamond skies
now, we're plucking petals
like promises
and watching them burn,
speaking evil truths
with deceitful tongues,
no fear or sadness left

(*we are wisps of smoke and fading breaths*)

darkness drips,
painting blood shadows
that writhe and whisper,
a burning example of the ache
that lives behind
our screaming eyes

we are startle shook,
cold and ashen,
plagued by fear,
the victims
of an animalistic haunting
that preys on our weaknesses
until we're left in pieces

(we've been buried alive in our own minds)

a twist of maybe and might,
of dark and light,
just the right amount of possibility
to make us lower our walls,
a slick serpent's kiss of wonder and awe,
one s ʟ o w motion step away
from a heart-dropping fall

(*wait for the plunge*)

ghostly whispers move
under a voodoo blood moon,
a slow-shimmer-slink
of air over bone,
their dark love calling us home,
cosmic cadavers
with claws that sink deep,
burning nerves
and setting veins on fire
we stand on the cusp of shadows,
slowly disappearing into the ether

(our souls are chained to a sinking sun)

charmingly deceptive,
innocence covering up
the sting of something dangerous

they move like waifs in the wind,
feather and bone creatures
with hunger
in their stares

they keep to the shadows,
dark souls stalking the shine
of those who bathe in the silver sun

they move through
the gloaming,
living with a secret
that'll soon devour them

(*even the ghosts are haunted*)

words stifled and choked down,
no escape of whisper or sound
as creativity is strangled by
a grapevine of twisted lies
and letters only barely exist
between sighs from parted lips,
every breath desiring to speak
piercing the night as silence screams

(there are nights the words won't come)

we came to a crossroads
lightning strikes right
and the desert looms left

you walk with me
into the storm
without a shred of fear

we've already been
to hell and back,
and we both know
there is nothing worse
than a lonely road
to a dark destination

we pass the raven
in a dress of lies,
the sheep in wolf's clothing,
the witch sipping on
the tears of her enemies,
the demon intensely watching
from the shadows

the weeks devolve
a spinning tangle of hours
a mess of minutes,
and inside

ashley jane

i am a chime of wrens,
all flight, no fight

i almost turn around,
but you
guide me through the doubt,
a slow movement forward
towards something lighter,
brighter,
more hopeful

we pretend to believe
that we're free
but
the rain left behind notes
our skin can remember,
and the thunder still beats
in frantic chords of
foreboding
even though a part of us
knew it was coming

you see,
it was never those monsters
we should be afraid of
the enemy within
is far more dangerous

(*quatervois*)

we called ourselves timeless
but time was never our friend
we felt our dreams fall
and love turn to ashes,
our hearts becoming prey
to the minute hand,
our lungs one breath away from collapse
time spied from the shadows
with merciless eyes
as we plunged towards darkness
time is a slow, soul-stealing incubus
that leaves us to wake up at ground zero

(*time is the devil on our shoulder*)

slow spinning magic,
medicated madness
marked by shadowy spells,
gruesomely gorgeous details
twisted up into abstract alchemy,
chaos taking center ring,
bloodless battles waged
in the deep wells of the mind

and it's over before it really begins,
dreaded truth settling
like stones beneath the skin

but then,
we already knew
all monsters were human

(*we already called this asylum our home*)

we traded alcohol for accolades,
swapped pills with the press of a button
we live in a temple of likes,
one push away from crumbling
and we can pretend all we want
that none of that matters
but here we are,
letting strangers and numbers
validate the way poetry sings within us

(the first step to recovery
is admitting you have a problem)

we reign over a time of wrongs,
vintage souls with porcelain hearts
wearing crowns made of maybes

we have always been
almost
perhaps
never quite so
never quite right
never the perfect time or place
(and see, still we cling
to the POSSIBILITY
that perfect even exists)

we are this inhalation of breathless skies,
all worry and weary and when and why
and i
am tired of letting go,
of moving on,
of floating through

it's tortuous,
being a ghost in a world
that doesn't belong to you,
watching over a world
that will never belong to you

(we float and flicker)

we dance with despair and sleep with fear,
our bodies weighed down
by tired hearts covered in glass shards

and we can't keep them from breaking
we can't keep them from crumbling,
from forming mountains of mourning
that our aching souls are too weary to climb

and our minds,
already heavy with worry,
are tied to a sinking stone,
buried way beneath the white cap waves
somewhere off the coast

and someone keeps telling us
to hold on
to be strong
to breathe deep
but our lungs are full of water,
and there is no life raft in sight

you see,
we never mastered the art of survival
we were too busy learning about fitting in,
knowing we never would

ashley jane

we were too busy learning how to drive
within the yellow painted lines
of the lanes we were told we belonged in

we walk in shoes that never fit us,
retracing the bitter footsteps of those
who will never know
what it's like to be held
in the cold hands of doubt,
who will never know
what it's like to feel
A L O N E

(this world is not our own)

we sit by the coast
channeling a calm we've never felt,
chasing a feeling that is far too fleeting
we barely exist,
a ghost, a carapace, a husk,
an E M P T I N E S S
floating over oceans,
as they re-teach us how to breathe

(*we learn from the seas*)

some days, i swear i don't know anything except that i have wounds blooming within me, bruises shaped like darkness and dahlias. i am more scars than skin, more dark than light, more silence than words, and yet, i'm still here. bruises and all. heavy heart and all. brittle bones and all. i am still here. some days, i don't know how to do anything except put one foot in front of the other and pray to reach my destination. some days, i can't get out of bed, and i am not sure if it is physical or mental or maybe, it is both. most days, i think my mind hates me. most days, i know my body hates me. but, i am still here. i am still here. I. AM. STILL. HERE.

(and that should count for something)

all darkness and dahlias

ashley jane

Danger

...let them go -- the
truthful liars and
the false fair friends
and the boths and
neithers -- you must let them go they
were born
to go...

e.e. cummings

you glide,
serpentine,
a sinister-slow-slither
on nights that shine,
all polished darkness and chaos divine
your eyes gleam with jealousy
as your fangs sink deep
and i am blood-stained,
bite marks blooming red on pale skin
while your poison seeps in
i am slipping into this forever after

(your shadows are calling me home)

eden beckons,

i n t o x i c a t i n g,
and we quickly descend into its depths,
its gilded-golden-glimmer
hiding a rose garden full of thorns
and a devil with a forked tongue
whispering lies beneath the apple tree
but i have learned,
there is no MERCY in your magic
there is no WISDOM in your words

(there is no soul in your sound)

he wears shades

of brimstone and damnation,
all burnished gold, falu and feuillemort
his eyes are home to a hidden world
made of ancient shadows and sunlight
they welcome you into the fire,
but you will not survive their invitation
to explore new depths
you will not make it through
their maze of night

(darkness lives within those flames)

his eyes are the shade
of illicit intentions,
and there is something shameless
in the taste of his lips
yet, here i am begging
for another dance with danger,
knowing destruction is inevitable

(*danger has dark eyes and a devilish smile*)

the devil stands
in his pressed suit,
holding two brass buttons,
offering them to you
as payment,
his pithy penance
for the sinking of your soul
HE WEARS DECEPTION
AS IF IT WERE DESIGNER

(*and he offers no returns*)

you were barrooms and bedroom eyes
filled with sweet nothing promises,
and i swallowed down your love
but couldn't handle the burn
it left me with a black heart
and a mouth full of ashes
and now i regret the way
i let you breathe me in
because your words
left bullet wounds and bruises
all over my skin
while those whiskey lips of yours
felt just like a razor's kiss

(i let you bleed me dry)

you like bending the rules,
as if they don't apply to you,
waging war with words that hurt

you build your piece de resistance
from the power you claim,
farming for fear
while ice runs in your veins,
using the shards in your heart
as a weapon for your
callously, cold coup de main

but, one day that'll change,
as parts begin to fall,
judgment, jenga style

(you aren't untouchable after all)

i once chased disaster
under bruised skies
and thought his kiss of chaos
tasted like love

he buried his heart behind walls
of concrete and glass,
and i foolishly thought
i could break them down

i was determined to be a lighthouse,
to guide him through the snowstorm,
but his soul was the cause
of that deathly cold,
and i was destined to freeze
in his icy touch

(*we cannot save them all*)

you taught me

we are all vicious at times
lingering somewhere in the red haze,
the part we call human
more monster than we care to admit
and sometimes
we are eyes that only know how to glare
and a mouth filled with blunt truths,
our tongues becoming swords drawn

you said that some days,
we are disconnected from the light,
that the darkness within us has been told
to stand up
and never back down

you said we can pretend
that we're all angels and innocence,
but somewhere beneath the pretense
we're all snakes
selling poison
in shiny apples

(honeycrisp or red delicious?)

fingers crossed behind their backs,
lips filled with whispered secrets,
eyes consumed by luck and lies,
the queen of hearts and the king of greed
rule in visions of verdigris,
the monarchy of anarchy
engulfed in a crown of flames,
all copper stained and weathered by chaos
they twist and bind our strings of fate,
mischief running rampant through their veins

(*we are caught in their reign of madness*)

they preach
slurred speeches
from drugged tongues
but they conquer nothing
they *rage, rage, rage,*
but it's all white noise
because lies cannot reach
these heights
and truth was never
their strong suit

(*their lips are moving, but i can't hear a word*)

*you paint in shades of jealousy
and wonder why the color
keeps seeping from your pages*

dreadful darkness I abhor,
dear bête noir,
painting pictures with words,
but your art is a lie,
the reckless ramblings
of the narcissistic nouveau,
driven by a compulsion to constantly show
that you're always better, smarter, more,
but you're the needle, damage done

(you're no flower, all thorn)

i'm not like you, with your fancy thoughts and your highbrow stare. i cannot pick words apart, carefully selecting only the best to serve. i tried, you know? to choose the perfect assortment. to arrange them in a way that would buy me favor. but i've learned that the taste of my poetry isn't refined enough for your picky appetite. *and i am ok with that.*

i saw your eyes,
barren of beauty,
colorblind to compassion,
hidden behind a cover of lies

you paint in brushstrokes of betrayal,
the ides of march in your dead stare,
words wielded like knives without care

you mean to cut deep,
tiger claws etching anger into pale skin

(your rage will never win)

do not be swayed
by her version of pretty
or the way she knows
all the right words to say
do not be tempted
by her beckoning shine
and the way her light professes
to know exactly where you should go
there is something deceptive
hiding behind all that praise,
something bitter behind
all that sweetness
do not follow her into the dark
her shimmer
won't lead you to safety
her fading flicker
won't guide you home
there is only falsity in her bones,
and the only place she knows
is a land of pretend

(*warning: danger ahead*)

her mouth is filled with danger,
lip gloss and bullets
collide with words that cut,
blow a kiss and fire a gun,
dirty secrets kept behind
doors sealed shut

(something dark lives within all that prettiness)

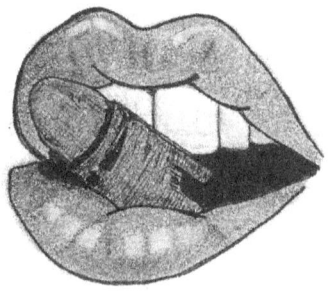

i am choking on the bitterness,
slipping down your spiral of spite,
tangled up in the sourness of words
i tried to sway you with honey,
but your teeth were made for biting

(*and i have fragile skin*)

they circle
like a shiver of sharks
out for blood,
determined to prove
that you
don't belong in their deep waters
they bare teeth
and stare
but there is nothing to fear
from paper tigers
who've forgotten
they're the ones
who don't belong
in the vast wonder
of your ocean

(*never let them get you down*)

some people give themselves far too much credit, believing that your world is somehow connected to theirs. or that you sit in wonder of them, when in actuality, they haven't crossed your mind since the time you said goodbye. it's like they need to feel that some attachment still exists to fill the emptiness that sits within themselves. they need to believe that they still play a role in your life. so, let them pretend to be the big bad that haunts you. you stopped fearing the monsters under the bed a long time ago.

i read your words
and all i can think about
is how bitter your tongue must taste
and i wonder how much it burns
as you spit them out

(*what's it like to choke on all that hate?*)

i am shrouded in your secrets,
drowning in your deadly spells,
destined to overdose
beside these cemetery ghosts
you see,
this caged heart beats
to the rhythm of catastrophes
while you whisper lies through your teeth
and i swallow them down,
distilled nuances brewed,
a little nip of always and forever
blended with a shuddering solitude
and a hint of the mind games
you so love to play,
a dash of lost longing
to hide the wilted wildflower taste,
and i ignore the silent screams,
words of caution carried
by the watchful breeze
slow - sip - slink
TOXIC
ARE
THE
TALES
I
DRINK

(it's all pretty poison in a coffee cup)

i read words of your misdeeds
scrawled in rushed ink
and tucked in the book with a crooked spine

i saw the sinister shadows stored on a shelf
beside the jar of hearts you've collected
from those pretty, posy, pastel dolls
weeping in the hall outside your room

i heard the midnight howls
and devilish laughs
that caused the silence to shatter
and the body to shake with tremors

i felt a jolt of fear from your phantom touch
like an electroshock from icy hands

i keep telling myself
that you were a bad dream,
but if ghosts don't exist
then who is the monster
at the foot of my bed

(and who is the demon lingering in the corner?)

you were dark magic rituals
on stormy winter nights,
a burning obsession with vengeance,
fire and ice colliding in a powerful spell

you led me,
like a lamb to the slaughter,
and i naively followed
but there was no pleasure in your pain,
no truth in the sorcery you spun

and now
you keep creating salt rings,
but your circle won't keep me out

(*you can't keep a good witch down*)

i saw darkness in your eyes,
razor blade rose petals
and black velvet lies,
platinum secrets
hiding behind walls
of stone and smoke
that faded and crumbled
each time you spoke
and it took magic to untangle
all the stories you told,
each reluctant truth
leaving me cold,
until the thrill of destruction
was wiped from your face,
and all that remained
was an empty soul swimming in a burning sea
and a venomous heart that i'll ignite in effigy

(strike a match and watch it burn)

ashley jane

i saw us again,

haunted faces in a wavering reflection,
misplaced hearts staring out
from a watery realm
we are sea billows and angry waves
we keep fighting - crashing - raging,
searching for flickers of warmth
on the ocean floor,
knowing moments of treasure
can be found
in between the madness
and the melancholy
and the messiness
but your sharks are circling again,
teeth bared and ready
and i am so very tired
of swimming against your current,
of suffocating beneath your surface,
of sinking into your seas
i'm just
so
very
tired

(*there is only weariness in my bones*)

your sun-bleached memories linger
like ghosts in the attic,
little stories floating
through the hallways
and sticking like spiderwebs
in the catacombs of my mind

they are no less haunting than the wind
whispering your name
or the blurred edges
of a beautiful dream
playing on refrain

i walk the veil
between death and life,
between beginnings and endings,
between knowing and forgetting
but the darkness returns
as it always does

october descends from the shadows,
and i am reminded
that my bones are a graveyard
decorated with the remnants of you,
all cracking paint and chipped stone,
leaves for the leaving
drifting from the tallest trees

ashley jane

i write your elegy in the dust
as tomorrow fades into today,
an effort to exorcise
any pieces that remain

i am tired of reading your rites
each morning
only to have you
rise again each night
please,
this time,
JUST
STAY
BURIED

(pretty please)

your voice
is seared into my mind,
a shrill sound
like when angels scream
and devils dance
and it is one decibel away from
UNBEARABLE

it calls from within,
challenging my last stand
against you,

and every damn word
tastes like poison

i can still see your smirk
and that look you give,
your pitch black
soul-haunting stare
stealing my breath
EVERY.SINGLE.TIME.

and I'm left gasping,
choking on a memory,

my tenuous grip on sanity
one slip away from broken

and with these flashbacks
you prove
that not all monsters
live in the shadows

you walked under the sun,
eyes gleaming
and a smile on your face
and yet
you're far worse
than any demon
i've met
in the dark

(*not all darkness is nocturnal*)

slow-slink-slither

he watches from the tree shadows,
beneath the leaves where apples grow
eden's temptation sitting sweetly
in the palm of his hand
we bite our prize,
but this knowledge
sitting on the tip of our tongue
tastes more like poison
than promise land
we scurry like mice,
hurrying to paradise
but we're swept back by his
tormented winds
UNRELENTING
OBSESSED
BRUTAL
POSSESSED
we are caught,
ravens in a birdcage
made of bones
the devil stalks the land
morphing all the gorgeous greens
into shades of rust and scarlet sand

(*i call this the beginning of the end*)

your version of peace only ever gave rise to tragedy

the years accumulate,
filling the space between us
we live in the margins,
avoiding shallow waters
filled with hollow words
we're all fake smiles
and bitter reminders
and thinly veiled distaste,
the ghosts of what once was
i suppose
i always thought
we'd find our way back
but apparently
some bridges
were made to burn

(*ours was made to burn*)

she swallowed your deceit,
duplicity filtering in through clenched teeth,
truth camouflaged behind lying eyes
her quiet pleas for honesty denied
by the rule breaker with ice in his veins,
the type of slick charmer
soft hearts want to embrace
but, now, she wields revenge like a gun,
whiskey on her lips
retribution on her tongue

(*she will come for you*)

this mouth of mine
is a well of waiting words,
all clever clapbacks
and a tongue made for cutting,
steel-edged, deliberate,
dissertation-dissections

you always told me to speak up,
right before you silenced me
so i have patiently crafted this blade
just. for. you.

(*shhhhh*)

ties that bind

--- BROKEN ---
we cut the string,
burned the rope,
severed the cord
we are a myth,
figments of something
now burned to ashes,
remnants in the dust

(some things weren't meant to last)

i breathe your words

some
taste of bitter betrayals
others
are lost in translation,
caught somewhere
in the void between
what is
and what should be

your whispers have melted
on my tongue,
EVOCATIVE
REDOLENT
POWERFUL

they scratch at my throat
i swallow them down,
invoking your name
my demon
my darling
dressed in the finest darkness

i am adrift in lace lies,
consumed by cashmere chaos,
bathed in the shadows
of this midnight maddening

you only know
the flavor of my
FRAGILITY
perhaps it is time
you take a sip of my
STRENGTH

(drink up)

all darkness and dahlias

Darkness

People will do anything, no matter how absurd, in order to avoid facing their own souls. One does not become enlightened by imagining figures of light, but by making the darkness conscious.

Carl Jung

she is the storm
that comes through,
so beautiful
and powerful
that no one
seems to notice
the destruction
that follows

(there is nothing calm about her)

she wears darkness well,
her dark coils of time
pressing us forward,
leaving only shadowed names
written on a crumbling wall

(find us in the rubble)

she is legend and myth,
dangerous encounters in the depths
leaving you gasping for air
between bound breaths
she is a shipwrecked treasure
calling your name,
so much art in the chaos
of her hurricane,
and you won't hesitate to sacrifice,
tempest tossed in the storm
of her restless nights,
tangled up in the waves
of one so heartless
that she'll leave you
sinking,
drowning
in her darkness

(watch us slip a little deeper)

do you feel it —
the chill in her veins,
the darkness that clings to her
when the night breaks?
she is blurred lines and wicked games
all witchery and magic and sin,
a conspiracy of ravens
living under her skin
and a soul dressed up
in macabre masquerade

(*do you remember now?*
you were the one who made her this way)

slip-slide voodoo

tracing pathways
in my brain,
a slow-motion serenade
and i'm at a loss
this melody
veering too far off course

(*it's all jumbled noise*)

i am dagger drunk
on bitter words
that deftly sink and slice,
horror and malice in every strike

(*this beast within my beauty
has always had a thing for knives*)

purple stained and sanguine
midnight dripping with time

my heart still hides
far away from where you seek

follow the moths
to the center of my soul
if you truly wish to know me

search the shadows for a downfall
and I'll be blooming,
entwined in the vines of a million dahlias

(find me swimming in petals of madness)

i am knee deep in shadows,
soil and bone planted
in unfamiliar ground
i bloom beneath roaring skies,
somewhere between
the orchids and the opium,
in the place where madness flows
within the roots
of a hollow heart possessed
with pretty poisons dressed
like delusion in the mind,
like dysfunction in the blood,
i am a conjurer of chaos

(can you count the shades of my darkness?)

i am darkened rooms and empty shelves,
undiscovered by someone else,
footsteps falling on unsteady ground,
memories that never need to be found

i am sunlight pouring in after the rain,
the sweet relief that follows the pain,
a song that shatters your frozen heart,
melting away every stinging shard

(*i am the gray in-between*)

she is a garden
of glass bones,
towering tomes
of private poems
written all over her skin,
veiled threats etched in
between the lines,
so sinister sublime

her touch
leaves you on
the verge of destruction,
an addiction crawling
deep within your veins
as you curse her name

(*but you can never get enough of her poison*)

queen of hearts,
of souls, of words
that cut without warning,
of shadows that blind
and storms that blow

(*don't let her swallow you whole*)

i play with fire,
clothe it in paper slips
filled with too many words,
give it sips of gasoline

i pause
and revel in its heat
all those pretty lies dressed in lace
make for such a brilliant blaze

(*let. them. burn.*)

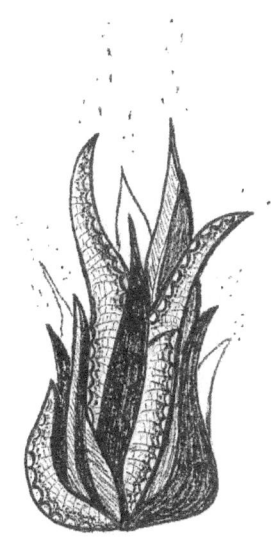

i climbed to the rooftop
searching for answers

i listened to the night whisper,
echoes from the future
telling me to leave and never look back

i think i believed you could be my lungs,
but those voices warned me
i would suffocate if i stayed in your reach

so, i packed it all up,
photographs and trinkets tucked away
in boxes labeled 'over'

AND I RAN

but some demons
bury themselves in your bones,
and no amount of distance
can stop the way they leave you
gasping

(*these memories won't let me breathe*)

rain kisses the dirt,
and i am slipping sideways,
falling out of time,
swallowed up by the fog
and a strange feeling
that leaves me undone

the clouds are leaking shadows,
waking the stranger within,
heralding the queen of darkness
and her tribe of graveyard ghosts

i dance with her secrets
in the eye of the storm
i cry tears of lightning
and embrace the thunder
raging inside

you offer up sympathy
for the devil i've become,
but this madness
was custom fit for me

(*these shadows made a home in my bones*)

i move down haunted halls,
following a path of echoes
it is lined in crimson,
in ivory bones and jet-black coals
i feel the hungry spirits
gnawing on my nerves
while my own heart pounds
within its cage

i hear the hurried flutter
of a million wings,
midnight moths
and a cauldron of bats
disturbed by every gasp of breath,
such a haunting melody it makes
as they escape

outside,
the red moon shines
unleashing the dead
they rise from damp earth
whispering my name

i watch the ghost
with the crooked smile
and the chilling gaze,
wicked written all over his face

ashley jane

he blends in with the shadows,
such a beautiful nightmare
hiding just out of site,
picking poisons
from a garden of weeds
while the night drips darkness

i can taste it,
the night
and the poison,
all anguished cries
and desperate pleas
and the cruel kiss
of an ending
i should've seen coming

(*the end is nigh*)

once,

i cradled the soul's sunlight
in my hands
i waded through cotton clouds
and swam in blue skies
i let them color my world,
then bottled it up
and got drunk on every shade

but their shimmer has faded
it is water-drenched and washed away,
hidden like a secret
in the box under my bed
and i am sober,
haunted,
drowning in vintage gray

(*i am one breath away from black*)

we fall violent beneath their gaze,
becoming the monsters
that lurk under our skin,
feral and uncaged,
fueled by venomous rage

(*we are all darkness and sin*)

they drip
down your chin,
rivulets so saccharine

(we pretend to loathe the gore)

knives dressed up in velvet
but the blade still stings

love, lies, lullabies
all so crimson sweet
they stain the tongue

grasp-gasp-gone

(*clean up when you're done*)

ashley jane

pricked by the thorns,
they bleed
in hidden passages,
victims locked away
behind concrete minds
they chase after phantoms
dispensing a death by cure,
modern medicine laced
with a hovering high
30 minutes, hours, days
they fade,
shackled-shattered-splintered,
they risk it all
because what doesn't kill you
S E T S Y O U F R E E

(*but these ghosts don't have the cure you need*)

an elixir

like pills and nightshade,
dopamine swallowed down
with champagne,
romance and roses
sitting on broken tables,
emotional blackmail in a pretty vase

we are the vandals of our own hearts,
carefully caged in a prison
of our own creation

we are lovesick
and looking for a fix
that can't be found in a bottle

(there is no cure for this disease)

these tell-tale hearts of ours
have a cellar filled with madness
and demons that rap-rap-rap
against the door

i dip my head beneath bubbles
laced with smoke and magic,
swim within the obscure,
dive into puddles of darkness
i rise with a smile that hides
a chamber of loaded words
these lips are a loaded gun

(...*bang*)

ashley jane

we've become masters

in honey coated lies,
our pathological lips
spilling venom in disguise
as we fire words without warning
and pretend it's okay,
darkness dressed up

(*we're all bullets and bouquets*)

quick slip slice,
paper torn
letter opener precise

the words are spilling out
in shades of night

they stir the soil
plant themselves
become jimsonweed
in your sip of tea

(can you taste the abyss?)

ashley jane

scarlet fever crashing
through blue veins,
ephemeral nights now crimson stained
with ruby roses and leather cuffs
(the sting is a drug, but it's never enough)

she searches for answers in the shadows,
stop motion stutter and start again,
gently tracing the map on her skin
(can you follow the path of her scars)

there's a taste of darkness
in her mercurial heart

(she's one cut away from falling apart)

i once swallowed shots
of the abyss
and chased it with red wine,
bitter and euphoric
and not the least bit satisfying

i let the california sunshine
sit quietly on my tongue,
followed its path
of milk and honey
into a world undone
into a mind UNDONE

i chased an amethyst aubade
with pearls of indigo ecstasy,
crawled into the hollow
and looked straight into
the eye of the beast
i became the beast

i became the shadows
stranded on the dark side of beauty
where a light like yours
could never go

(*i made it my home*)

chills

shoot like arrows
beneath the skin,
drawn deeper into veins
that still remember my name,
to a heart still iced over
from the last time i came

i stay in the dark,
a glowing ghost,
a white wisp whisper
that haunts your days
and steals your nights,
leaving you shaking
and aching
and cold

―

you've got to learn how
to protect your soul

(*don't let my shadows take hold*)

i am caught out of orbit,
swept up in this
downpour-deluge of
D E S T R U C T I O N
(can you taste the chaos?)

we are
itchy fingers on a
quick-trigger-hand-grenade,
minds dancing with delight
at the cold, dark danger,
mouths filled with yesterday's ghosts
—
isn't it
masterful,
the way madness
befalls the weary?

(tales of the tired and tumultuous)

ashley jane

i am caged
in chaos and change,
bleeding in shades
of anarchy red,
tethered to
the slow creation
of something new
as pages are torn
into brackens of
blackened thorns
that leave scratched
ink glyphs of
insanity's truth
behind every
crevice, rock and vine
where petals grow
within seconds of time
i am the frenzy and the fury
known as madness's muse

(i'm coming for you)

*a collaboration with Matt Shirley

dark clouds slice
through colored skies,
calling out to veins
bleeding rain and ink,
searching the surface of bones
now caked in dust and ashes and decay,
the only remnants of memories
that i set ablaze

i am a disheveled mess of uncertainty,
hushed nights in haunted rooms
that may be abandoned
but are far from empty

i weep with willows in the shadows

sadness clings to the air
reach out,
and you'll touch grief
listen,
and you'll hear sorrow

(*do you taste the melancholy?*)

i'm a black hole reaching out,
pulling you in to this emptiness
that runs in my veins,
hoping that you'll be the light
that pushes that darkness away

i've become
too many shades of gray,
uneven lines and dark circles
where shadows lurk
beneath the surface
with those black skies
only you can paint blue

i am begging for release,
aching cries
that only you can silence

(*won't you give me your hand?*)

all darkness and dahlias

Disillusioned

The world breaks everyone
and afterward
many are strong at the broken places.

Ernest Hemingway, A Farewell to Arms

wilted,

like funeral roses
and the darkest of dahlias,
black edges crumbling
from the weight of your ghost
they sit in stagnant denial,
thoughts swirling
and dreams drowning
in their desolation
until petals are plucked
and seeds are strewn

perhaps
they'll create
a garden of heartache
for all the lonely people
to water

(perhaps then we won't be so lonely)

you've never really known
what it is to burn,
the blaze of a glaring sun
scorching its way across your shadows,
the fiery flame of darkness
scratching at your skin

you've never felt the claw marks
of demons desperate for release

you've never heard the whispered pleas
between talking spirits and heavy hearts
that live oceans away and mountains apart

you use your amulets and trinkets and faith,
avoiding the apple and the serpent,
keeping yourself clear of the heat

i wonder how it feels
to be so well-contained

(*what is it like to live with peace in your veins?*)

we preach
of peace on earth,
talk of reason and reflection,
scream fire and flame into the vast void
until only singed echoes of us remain

we spill words that we don't believe,
stand hypnotized by the lights
of phosphene dreams,
makes up stories of immortal lives
(the less they know, the easier it is to pretend)

we walk these jagged edges,
jump from blind heights,
chase salvation in things
(and people)
that will never wash our souls clean,
and when we're asked to define anything

we falter
we filter
we flee

(*fickle hearts should not be trusted*)

we have lost ourselves
somewhere along the way,
dreams of peace stolen
to make room for war,
cards on the table,
battles waged
to settle old scores

we file away grievances
and write hate on the wall,
etching our demands
in ink black and blood red,
like angry urban scrawl

we toss out hostile words
from behind enemy lines
as we exchange compassion
for indifference,
cries of help now denied
by vicious minds
and shallow hearts

(*we are a world of beauty swallowed up by the dark*)

we hover

between graceful ruin
and withered decay,
brave heart beauties
in a vicious cycle
of colliding
and breaking apart

we are here, then gone,
lost, then found,
our night souls bathed in
blinding white,
captured in pools
of lighthouse shine

we are
u n c o v e r e d,
treasure pillaged
from the collapse

we are the spoils
of a war
we never wanted
to be a part of

(*it rages on behind our eyes*)

ashley jane

light barely peeks through
from the shadows of a shrouded sun,
and we wait
until the night swarm stains the sky
we watch like voyeurs
from darkened corners,
caught up in the masquerade
we use blackmail
to earn our way behind the veil
we traipse through dead forests,
scurrying through
the twists and turns,
eager to bury our bones
alongside the ghosts
that dance on our souls
we covet their freedom

WE SINK

WE METAMORPHOSE

WE FLOAT

(*we are nothing more than dust in the wind*)

we strike a match and let it blaze,
better at destruction
than we ever were at healing

we are bullets and bonfires,
violets and verdigris,
pretty ghosts
with a penchant for poisoning
EVERY. LITTLE. THING.

we hold false hopes with rough hands,
feeding the masses
with mischievous intent

we don't have the answers,
but we like to pretend
even though
it only makes things worse

(*but we've always loved watching things burn*)

ashley jane

we exist in this drifting dark,
haunted whispers within the walls
of abandoned rooms,
carefully concealed horrors
stored behind boarded windows
and locked doors

we slink into the shadows
of serpentine dreams,
waking the night from its slumber

we rise from the ashes
of burnt offerings,
desperate for just one sip
of the fire that once raced in our veins

(*we keep chasing disaster*)

you keep locking yourself away in the dark as if your shadows need to hide. as if you don't deserve to shine. but you want to. i can feel it in my bones. i know it's easy to give up. but you've got to learn how to break down those walls of yours if you ever want the light to get in.

anger stained with blood red rage,
their hearts beat a gunpowder ballad
while their mouths spill silence and bombs
ashes drip from their lips
chaos spills from their fingertips
they are unhinged danger
laced with fake calm,
and we can pretend
but peace is gone with the wind,
finding hell without a sound
we steadily cling to hope
while the world is spinning upside down

(*we must find a way to turn things around*)

we've never been good
at sharing the burdens we carry,
our guilty hearts
determined to spare those
more innocent than ourselves

we walk the road to purgatory,
but we walk it alone,
a wolf separated from the pack
because some battles
cannot be fought together
some battles stain gentle souls

this world is a cruel place
held together by rough hands
that only know how to leave bruises

we've just been fortunate enough
to learn how to escape,
how to break free

we move fluid, like water,
racing towards a dying sea

we rush past the shallows
for we are songbirds of the deep,
singing our sorrow as we sink

do you see us drifting?
do you see us drowning?
do you see the heaviness
WEIGHING

us

DOWN?

(we are going under)

we wake up
and turn on the television,
knowing we'll be greeted by
something somber,
something that defies logic,
something that turns our stomachs
because it's an everyday thing now,
this dark world filled with people
we no longer recognize

they are brittle bones
and empty hearts,
blind eyes and shallow souls

we switch off the television,
wavering between disgusted
and disheartened

we get dressed
and go out into the world,
determined not to become
like them,
determined to prove
that goodness and kindness
still exists
in us

(*because it must*)

humanity is lost

somewhere between the bullet holes
and the children's screams,
(those of us with hearts
are calling out to set them free)

i think the roots between us
are buried far too deep
we no longer remember
what connected us,
our eyes too blind to see
that we are caught up in the crossfade
of this distorted mirror reality,
our perspective skewed
by fiction presented as facts

i fear that we'll soon reach the breaking point

(*there is no going back*)

we sought escape

from a war we weren't a part of

but there is nowhere to run

when the dark has made a home

within us all

ashley jane

the time to have patience has passed,
swept up in the thoughts and prayers
that we pretended would save us

there is a place for faith and its ties to strength,
but hope and well wishes haven't changed a thing

gunshots still ring out in the silence,
and innocent hearts are stained with violence
while we tuck it all away for another day

(my heart beats an ache:
it's not okay, it's not okay, it's not okay.)

enough is E N O U G H.

(*it's time to wake up*)

we are sunken ruins,

blank pages and endless words
buried somewhere in the deep,
beautiful shipwrecks filled with agonies
immortalized in spilled ink

we sleep beneath
sneaking waves
as they trespass
across a graveyard of aches,
carrying old memories,
nostalgia crashing into deadly shores

we scream our pain
into the ocean's roar,
and it is swallowed whole

we exist in this anxious solitude,
our poetry consumed

(*maybe the sea will save our souls*)

we are the dusk settling into the land,
our hands reaching into the ether
to tie back the hands of day

we are born and raised
by low lights and lush shadows,
by good and evil and all the dreams
that live in between

we are seekers of sight,
traveling vast pathways
of wandering wisdom,
determined to put down roots in places
that have never seen the sun's shine,
that have never known serenity
because chaos is only thing that grows
in cities covered by cobwebs

we preach peace on corners
where hate hangs thick in the air
because we know
that broken things can be mended
if we all learned to speak
in a language
that sounds more like
L O V E

(*less hate. more love.*)

rust stains

on innocent hands,
a tender sorrow washed away
by the rain,
proclaimed clean,
but the pain is still there

we were wildflowers in eden,
pristine, lovely little things
now, tragedy clings
to petals afraid of falling
—
sometimes,
there is beauty in letting go
hope is the wind
that will carry us home

(we wait for the breeze to catch us)

stop chasing after things that destroy you. you don't have to drown in crashing waves. there are beautiful places to explore on dry land.

shine-bright-shimmer,
a sharp cut of light ricocheting
off chandeliers of crystal ice

we follow its warning,
shards of frosted ink
scrawled across the sky,
foreboding written out
in this HOLY SILENCE,
telling of how darkness still lingers
in the hallows from where we came

hope is fleeting,
but we will not turn back
the stars will be our lighthouse

(*the moon will carry us through*)

we spent most our last days
bound in
tangled threads of treason,
chained by serpents
with lies on their tongues
and venom in their hearts
their sting aches
and their teeth are sharp
and the reflection of their soul
is mirror black
they believed us weak
and breakable,
but we fought back

(*we will always fight back*)

all darkness and dahlias

i bloom best in shadows,

all darkness and dahlias

hiding from

your prying eyes

all darkness and dahlias

Acknowledgements

To my other half, who motivates me and reassures me and reminds me that sleep is important when I go without for days. You are my rock. Love you always.

To my family and friends who continue to support me even though poetry is not their cup of tea. It means so much. Thank you.

To Nadiya and Angie for their amazing art skills. To Gypsy for proofing and editing. To Alfa, for your unending guidance, friendship and shoulder to lean on. To all of the SagePoets for being such an incredible tribe.

To my readers, I am so grateful for your continued support. You are all amazing!

If you like this book, or any of my published works, please leave a review. And if you take photos, share them with me on any of my social media or email. I would love to see and share them!

Other books by this Author:

Love. Lies and Lullabies

The Mums are Filled with Melancholy

About the Author

Ashley Jane is an indie author from Alabama. She is a former Inmate Substance Abuse Counselor with research published in Crime and Delinquency magazine. She has also been featured on various poetry sites. Currently, she moves between consulting and editing books for others. She still enjoys research, and you'll often find her alternating between reading poetry books and psychological studies.  She loves concerts and traveling, especially anywhere tropical. She lives with her husband and their one child, a rescue cat named Shadow Monkey.

When not working or writing, you can find her running prompts and pages on social media. She is the founder and co-host of FallsPoetry prompt, which runs on both Instagram and Twitter. She also co-hosts DarkLines and DrugVerse prompts on Twitter.

Find Me on Social Media

Web: www.breathwords.com

Facebook: www.facebook.com/breathwords

Instagram: @breathwords

Twitter: @breathwords

Pinterest: www.pinterest.com/breathwordspoems

Tumblr: @breathwords

Vero: @breathwords

Mirakee: @breathwords

Lettrs: @breathwords (#635005)

Poetizer: Ashley Jane (breathwords)

Email: breathofwordspoems@gmail.com

About the Illustrator

Angie Shea is an artist and writer from Atlanta, GA. She works in a variety of mediums and styles, including pen and ink illustration. Her poetry and art are available to view on Instagram and Facebook. She has been featured in poetry anthologies, and she is currently working on her first poetry collection.

Facebook: a.shaewriter
Instagram: a.shea_writer

For more of her art,
follow her on Instagram at: a.shea_artist

www.ingramcontent.com/pod-product-compliance
Lightning Source LLC
Chambersburg PA
CBHW071201070526
44584CB00019B/2872